American Piano Classics

39 Works by Gottschalk, Griffes, Gershwin, Copland and Others

Selected and with an Introduction by
Joseph Smith

DOVER PUBLICATIONS, INC.
Mineola, New York

ACKNOWLEDGMENTS

For access to scores and related materials, and for their kind cooperation throughout the editorial process, thanks are due to the following institutions and individuals:

Music Division of the New York Public Library for the Performing Arts, the Astor, Lenox, and Tilden Foundations; Schomburg Center for Research in Black Culture, New York Public Library; Library of the New England Conservatory of Music; The Sibley Music Library, Eastman School of Music; Music Division of the Library of Congress; and to John Davis, Dr. Edward A. Berlin, Dr. Jean E. Snyder, and Severo M. Ornstein.

Bibliographical Note

This Dover edition, first published in 2001, is a new compilation of works originally published separately in early authoritative editions. Joseph Smith's introduction was prepared specially for this collection. Minor corrections in the music have been made without comment.

International Standard Book Number: 0-486-41377-2

Manufactured in the United States of America
Dover Publications, Inc., 31 East 2nd Street, Mineola, N.Y. 11501

CONTENTS

An alphabetical list of titles appears on p. 170.

INTRODUCTION

Where European countries boast long, continuous musical traditions, America boasts diversity. Our heritage is derived from countries on every continent, and is composed of a wealth of varied social influences, folk sources, historical backgrounds, and traditions. And so is our music. What is American music? This collection may not give an answer, but at least it offers 39 different answers, from the Civil War era to the early 1920s.°

Despite his tragically early death at 38, **Stephen Collins Foster** wrote about 200 songs. Some—like "My Old Kentucky Home"—are so thoroughly absorbed into the American consciousness that we tend to think of them as folk songs. Both "The Village Bells Polka" and "Santa Anna's Retreat" (commemorating Zachary Taylor's victory over the great Mexican general in 1847), like Foster's songs, show how he could create potent melodies in the absence of harmonic sophistication.

Louis Moreau Gottschalk proved to an astounded Europe that "American pianist" was not an oxymoron. The first composer to base a body of work on African-American and Caribbean material, he produced a series of elegant yet rousing bravura pieces. Their rhythmic ostinatos and florid figurations are aimed directly at the listener's nervous system. (The coda of "The Banjo," incidentally, quotes "Camptown Races" by his close contemporary Stephen Foster.)

Born a slave, the young **"Blind Tom"** (Bethune) was first exhibited as a musical prodigy by his master in 1857. He had absolute pitch, the phenomenal ability to repeat pieces on a single hearing, and struck the American public as strange and miraculous. "Water in Moonlight," from Blind Tom's teen years, is typical of the sweetly naive style of his compositions. The original title page bore the introduction, "Tom will now give you his idea of a great lake in the moonlight."

The first group of American concert composers sprang from late-19th-century Boston. These musicians, generally European-trained, brought a new earnestness and technical sophistication to American music, as well as a reverence for traditional forms and techniques. **John Knowles Paine** was America's very first professor of music—the man who made music theory classes an American academic tradition. In his "Birthday Impromptu," the enigmatic dedication "à mon ami," with its pointing finger and low F on the staff, refers to Paine's friend Farlow—the birthday celebrant. Thus the pun: "*Fa*-low."

Arthur Foote was particularly admired for his polished chamber music. The fourth of his *Five Poems* for piano inspired by the words of Omar Khayyám is a romantic musing on the famous quote: "*. . . a jug of wine, a loaf of bread—and thou.*"

While pursuing a formidable academic career—including a 30-year stint as director of the New England Conservatory of Music—composer **George W. Chadwick** produced appealingly fresh, rhythmically alive music. Like his splendid orchestral works, the sardonic "Scherzino" proves a happy exception to generalizations about Bostonian staidness.

Edward MacDowell's once-universal anointment as "America's first great composer" is disputable, but his melodic charm, ardor, and individuality are not. Even those who feel that his sonatas sometimes fall short of their ambitions may rejoice in his wealth of adorable miniatures, which are naive in the best sense of the word. "The Joy of Autumn" romps through an array of rapidly changing virtuosic textures.

The Bostonian group regarded **Amy Beach** as "one of the boys," and she shared their aesthetic although she was virtually self-taught as a composer. The bird calls preserved in her Op. 92 pieces are "exact notations of hermit thrush songs, in the original keys but an octave lower, obtained at the MacDowell Colony, Peterborough, New Hampshire"—her frequent summer home following extensive European tours as pianist-composer. She wanted this music to be "*very* free," with "*excessive* rubato," and with the bird songs standing out in sharp relief from all else.

Like the Bostonians a half-century earlier, Nebraskan **Howard Hanson** also functioned happily within European traditions and flourished in academe. Listening to his sweeping,

°While I have included "popular" as well as "concert" works, I've chosen only from pieces that were composed to be performed as written, without requiring improvisation. One further exclusion should be acknowledged: Charles Ives was active during the years represented here, but copyright restrictions prevent his inclusion.

lush orchestral music, one would never imagine he could compose the bracingly lean and clattering "Clog Dance."

Composer, conductor, and virtuoso cellist **Victor Herbert** is best remembered today for his delectible forty-some operettas including such perennials as *Babes in Toyland, Naughty Marietta,* and *The Red Mill.* It is a tribute to his remarkable craft that, although by his own admission a "rotten" pianist, he could write such idiomatic piano pieces as the teasing "La Coquette" and the pensive "Indian Summer."

Ethelbert Nevin's aesthetic is so dated that descriptions of his music must revert to the language of his day—"refined". . . "graceful" . . . "lilting". . . "delightful." Nevin often used European idioms for picturesque effect, but in "At Home (June Night in Washington)" the picturesque elements are African-American—imitations of banjo and male quartet.

Over and over, **Scott Joplin** managed to invest the circumscribed rag form with an astounding variety of texture and mood, as the four beautifully differentiated strains of "Fig Leaf" attest. Joplin proved that ragtime syncopation can as effectively express gentleness and lyric warmth as it can animal energy. His gifted and original protégé **Joseph Lamb**, had a special penchant for dense sonorities and "dark" keys. His wistful "Ragtime Nightingale" uses motifs from Chopin's "Revolutionary" Etude and Nevin's "Nightingale Song," not as quotations but as threads woven into the fabric of the piece.

James Reese Europe, who toured with the legendary dance team of Irene and Vernon Castle, was not just a ragtime bandleader—he was a cultural leader. In his 1912 Carnegie Hall concert, a 115-piece orchestra drawn from his Clef Club for black musicians forced the New York public to consider African-American music as art rather than merely entertainment. Europe and his co-conductor **Ford Dabney** would develop their collaborative compositions by four-handed piano improvisation. The choice of 5/4 for "Castles' Half and Half" is an example of the team's adventurousness.

"Rialto Ripples," a 1917 collaboration between 19-year-old **George Gershwin** and pianist-songwriter **Will Donaldson**—like Gershwin's posthumous "Novelette in Fourths"— anticipated the "novelty" idiom of the 1920s. This style continued to influence Gershwin's serious piano writing in his *Rhapsody in Blue,* the three *Preludes,* and even such a grand, romantic work as his *Concerto in F.* Derived from ragtime, the novelty style exults in its own trickiness—it subverts meter with extended hemiola, revels in double notes, and often features wordplay in its titles. In the prototypal "Kitten on the Keys," **Zez Confrey** found the ideal programmatic image for this exhibitionistic style.

Antonín Dvořák came to New York in 1893 to serve as director of New York's National Conservatory of Music (and gave us his beloved Symphony "From the New World"). From this pulpit he exhorted American composers to use African-American folksong as a source for American concert music. How appropriate that one of those who followed his advice should be **Harry T. Burleigh**—a scholarship student at the conservatory—the very individual who introduced Dvořák to spirituals. Burleigh went on to win success as a singer, song composer and arranger of spirituals. His "On Bended Knees" is part of *From the Southland,* his only piano work.

Henry T. Gilbert, an American pioneer in using African-American materials in orchestral concert music, is best remembered for his *Dance in Place Congo.* His *Negro Dances* are drawn from his unpublished operatic treatment of the *Uncle Remus* stories.

Native American melodies—monophonic and pentatonic—have tended to resist conventional European practices. **Arthur Farwell**, however, seemed able to let each tune guide him toward an appropriate and colorful treatment. His Wa-Wan Press—founded in 1901, and named after an Omaha Indian ceremony for peace, fellowship, and song—sought a new indigenous American music derived from ragtime, Native American music, and cowboy songs. This effort was as great an encouragement to his generation of composers as Henry Cowell's New Music edition would later be to a younger set.

There have been many pianist-composers and many rodeo cowboys, but only the Texan **David Guion** succeeded as both. It was his setting of "Home on the Range" that established it as the archetypal cowboy song. Guion recalled the tune of "Sheep and Goat" from his earliest memories of home and fiddlers' dances. He has thrown snatches of other cowboy breakdowns and some of his own "side-kicks" into this arrangement.

Following the elevated aspirations of the Boston school, the jaunty facetiousness of **John Alden Carpenter**'s ballets *Krazy Kat* and *Skyscapers,* as well as the present "Polonaise Américaine," seemed fresh, provocative—and modern. The compositions of **Eastwood Lane**, well known in their day, introduced home pianists to the pleasures of mildly "modern" nonfunctional harmony. (Jazz great Bix Beiderbecke cited Lane among his influences.) Of the present piece, Lane wrote: "All lovers of the Adirondacks will recall their first impression of this bird, its eerie, mournful cry and almost insane laughter. The Indians and guides regard the loon with superstitious awe: they believe that to injure or kill one means certain misfortune, and many are the stories told of the evil which befell those rash enough to harm one."

The music of **Charles Griffes** has a uniquely rapt, visionary quality, often achieved through hypnotic ostinatos and harmonic stasis; even when his descriptive titles and vaporous textures lead us to call him an impressionist, his style is distinct from those of Debussy and Ravel. The delicacy of his piano writing can often conceal some quite dissonant juxtapositions.

Leo Ornstein's early pieces—with titles like "Wild Man's Dance" and "Suicide in an Airplane"—represented (and may still represent) the *ne plus ultra* of pianistic violence. The composer once acknowledged that he often left blood on the keys! He arrived at this style, he said, through inner necessity, and that it at first "horrified me as much as it has since horrified others." Brief but brutal, Ornstein's "Dance of the Dwarfs" is as demanding metrically as it is pianistically.

Around the age of fifteen, **Henry Cowell** composed "The Tides of Manaunaun," discovering the technique that would remain indissolubly linked with his name—the "tone-cluster"—played with flat hand, fist, or forearm. In "Frisking," the hands are independent not only in regard to key, but also barline. Cowell's challenging techniques do not render his music difficult to appreciate, though—he is one of the most ingratiating of modernists. (Cowell, Ornstein, and even the short-lived Griffes, would go on to compose important, substantial works in styles utterly different from their early pieces.)

Of American composers working exclusively in "serious"

music, **Aaron Copland** remains the most celebrated. He managed to maintain his individual style both in difficult works admired by fellow musicians—like the masterly *Piano Variations*—and in accessible works that captivated the general public, like his ballets *Rodeo* and *Appalachian Spring*, and the stirring *A Lincoln Portrait* and *Fanfare for the Common Man*. Even his first published works show these two sides: the saucy "Cat and the Mouse," inspired by a La Fontaine fable, exemplifies the accessible Copland; the "Passacaglia" anticipates his austere works.

———————————

Is it really possible that Beach's romantic hermit thrush and Confrey's hyperactive kitten were born in the same year—1921? That 1912 saw Carpenter producing his witty polonaise, Griffes conjuring his elusive night wind, and Cowell using his forearm to make a tide? That, in 1914, as Gilbert was composing a dance in African-American style, Europe and Dabney were composing a dance in 5/4 time? Academics, wild iconoclasts, folklorists, purveyors of home music, concert composers borrowing popular idioms, popular composers borrowing concert idioms—all rub shoulders in these pages. *E pluribus unum.*

Joseph Smith
New York, Fall 2000

The *New York Times* called pianist Joseph Smith's playing "eloquent," and the *Frankfurter Allgemeine Zeitung* found him a "richly sensitive interpreter." He has performed and recorded works by many of the composers included in this volume, including the complete piano music of Charles Griffes. Smith is author of *Piano Discoveries* (Ekay Music), and editor of *Four Early 20th Century Piano Suites by Black Composers* (G. Schirmer). His articles on piano music have appeared in major periodicals, and his feature "Joseph Smith's Piano Bench" appears regularly on National Public Radio's *Performance Today.*

A Hermit Thrush at Morn

No. 2 of two "Hermit Thrush" pieces, Op. 92 (1921)

"I heard from morn to morn a merry thrush
Sing hymns of rapture, while I drank the sound
With joy."

J. Clare

Amy Beach
[*Mrs. H. H. A. Beach*]
(1867–1944)

* *These bird-calls are exact notations of hermit thrush songs, in the original keys but an octave lower, obtained at Mac Dowell Colony, Peterborough, N.H.*

1

Scottish Legend

No. 1 of *Two Compositions*, Op. 54 (1903)

Amy Beach

Lento con molto espressione.

Water in the Moonlight

(1866)

"Blind Tom" Bethune

(1849–1908)

On Bended Knees

No. 5 from the suite *From the Southland: Piano Sketches* (1907?)

Harry T. Burleigh
(1866–1949)

"Oh, I look away yonder—what do I see?
  A band of angels after me.
Come to tote me away from de fiel's all green
  'Cause nobody knows de trouble I've seen!"

Polonaise Américaine

(1912)

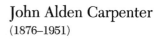

John Alden Carpenter
(1876–1951)

Allegro con moto (♩=92)

16

Scherzino

No. 3 of *Six Characteristic Pieces*, Op. 7 (1882)

George Whitefield Chadwick
(1854–1931)

The Cat and the Mouse

Scherzo Humoristique (1920)

after a La Fontaine fable

Aaron Copland
(1900–1990)

Kitten on the Keys

(1921)

Zez Confrey
(1895–1971)

Passacaglia

(1921–2)

Aaron Copland

The Tides of Manaunaun

Henry Cowell

EXPLANATION OF SYMBOLS

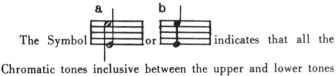 The Symbol _____ or _____ indicates that all the Chromatic tones inclusive between the upper and lower tones given, are to be played simultaneously.

Whole and half notes are written open, as in symbol (a).

Notes of other time values are written closed, as in symbol (b).

A sharp or flat above or below such a symbol indicates that only the black keys between the outer limits are to be played, while a natural in the same position indicates that only the white keys are to be played.

This rule is to be followed irrespective of key signature, since the tones within a tone-cluster are not affected by the key.

Only the outer tones, the highest and lowest, must be in conformance with the key signature.

It is seen therefore that the symbol [notation] stands

for [notation] all played together)

the symbol [notation] stands for [notation]

the symbol [notation] stands for [notation]

the symbol [notation] stands for [notation]

The tone clusters indicated by these symbols are to be played either with the flat of the hand, or with the forearm or with the fist, according to the length of the cluster.

Care should be taken to play all the tones exactly together, and in legato passages, to press down the keys, rather than to strike them, thus obtaining a smoother tone quality, and a unified sound.

Care must be taken that the outer limits of the clusters are absolutely precise, as written, and that each tone as indicated between the outer limits is actually sounded.

The forearm should be held in a straight line along the keys, except in case the arm of the pianist is too long, in which case the arm must be partly dropped off the keys at an angle, to give the proper length.

If desired, melody tones may be brought out with the knuckle of the little finger, in the playing of clusters.

Tone clusters to be played in the manner indicated by the symbol (◊) will be written as:

An arrowhead is used in connection with arpeggiation marks to indicate whether the arpeggiation is to be from the lowest tone upwards, as is customary, (↑) or from the highest tone downwards (↓).

R. F. Stands for right fist; L. F. for left fist.
R. A. Stands for right arm; L. A. for left arm.

The Tides of Manaunaun

No. 1 of *Three Irish Legends* (1912)

Story according to John Varian

Manaunaun was the god of motion, and long before the creation he sent forth tremendous tides,
which swept to and fro through the universe, and rhythmically moved the particles
and materials of which the gods were later to make the suns and the worlds.

Henry Cowell
(1897–1965)

Largo, with rhythm

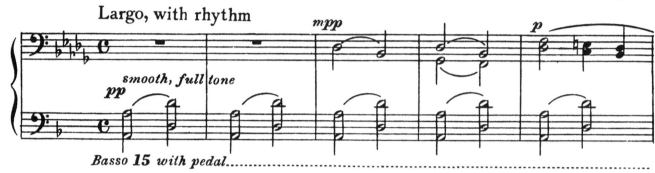

Frisking

No. 2 of *Nine Ings* (1916)

Henry Cowell

Vivo e leggiero M.M. ♪ : 144

Castles' Half and Half

(1914)

James Reese Europe (1881–1919)
& Ford T. Dabney (1883–1958)

FROM MESA AND PLAIN
Indian, Cowboy and Negro Sketches for Pianoforte
Op. 20 (1905)

Arthur Farwell
(1872–1952)

Navajo War Dance

Pawnee Horses

"There go the Pawnee horses. I do not want them—I have taken enough."

(Based on an Omaha melody sung by Francis La Flesche and transcribed by Edwin S. Tracy)

From the piano sketches *From Mesa and Plain*, Op. 20

Arthur Farwell

Prairie Miniature

(Based on the melodies of two Cowboy folk songs)

From the piano sketches *From Mesa and Plain*, Op. 20

Arthur Farwell

Wa-Wan Choral

"The clear sky, the peaceful earth is good, but peace among men is better."

(From the Wa-Wan ceremony of the Omahas; the melody from Alice C. Fletcher's "A Study of Omaha Indian Music,"
Peabody Museum, Cambridge)

From the piano sketches *From Mesa and Plain*, Op. 20

Arthur Farwell

Plantation Melody

(As recorded by Alice Haskell. Harmonized by Arthur Farwell.)

From the piano sketches *From Mesa and Plain*, Op. 20

Poem

"A Book of Verses, underneath the Bough,
A Jug of Wine, a Loaf of Bread—and Thou
Beside me singing in the Wilderness—
Oh, Wilderness were Paradise enow!"

No. 4 of *Five Poems (after the Rubaiyat of Omar Khayyám),* Op. 41 (1899?)

Arthur Foote
(1853–1937)

The Village Bells Polka

(1850)

Stephen Collins Foster
(1826–1864)

64

Santa Anna's Retreat
from Buena Vista

Quick Step (1848)

Stephen Collins Foster

Rialto Ripples

Rag (1917)

George Gershwin (1898–1937)
& Will Donaldson (1891–1954)

TRIO

D. S al Fine

Negro Dance No. 2

From *Negro Dances: Five Pieces for the Pianoforte* (1914)

Henry F. Gilbert
(1868–1928)

Note de l'Auteur

Je recommande pour ce petit morceau la plus scrupuleuse observation de ce qui est marqué. Le caractère d'ardeur à la fois mélancolique et inquiète que j'ai cherché à lui imprimer disparaîtrait entièrement, si l'exécutant ne s'attachait à donner aux rythmes qu'il renferme leur valeur exacte. La mélodie devra se détacher sur le fond tourmenté mais symetrique de la basse avec une sonorité "cantante" et une "morbidezza" qui sont les traits caractéristiques de la musique créole. Se mouvoir avec toute la désinvolture de = l'Ad Libitum= et du = tempo rubato= dans l'intérieur de la mesure, et ne point cependant en franchir les limites extrèmes, tel est le secret du charme que produit la musique des Antilles, et de la difficulté que présente ce morceau dont les mélodies et leur arrangement, bons ou mauvais, m'appartiennent entierement.

Note by the Author

I must suggest this little piece should be played exactly as it is written, as the license occasionally indulged in by pupils, of substituting their own thoughts for those of the composer, must inevitably interfere with the general effect. The characterestics of mingled sadness and restless passion which distinguish the piece would be utterly lost were not the accuracy of each changing rythm fully sustained. The melody should stand out in bold relief from the agitated but symetrical back-ground of the bass with the singing sonorousness and passionate languor which are the peculiar traits of Creole music. To give entire scope to the "Ad Libitum" and "Tempo Rubato" and at the same time not to transcend the extreme limits of the time, is the principal difficulty as well as the great charm of the music of the Antilles, from which I have borrowed the outline of this Composition, the Theme and Arrangement being exclusively my own. I intend hereafter, as a prelude to my pieces, to make a few observations on the proper method of playing them, hoping that those who like my music, may accept the fervent desire to facilitate its execution, as an acknowledgement of their kindly appreciation.

L.M. GOTTSCHALK.
New York 21 Juin 1862.

O, ma charmante, épargnez-moi!

"O, my charmer, spare me!": Creole Caprice (1861)

"The Author in this *morceau* (which is entirely original) has endeavored to convey an idea of the singular rhythm and charming character of the music which exists among the Creoles of the Spanish Antilles. Chopin, it is well known, transferred the national traits of Poland to his Mazurkas and Polonaises, and Mr. Gottschalk has endeavored to reproduce in works of an appropriate nature the characteristic traits of the Dances of the West Indias."

Louis Moreau Gottschalk
(1829–1869)

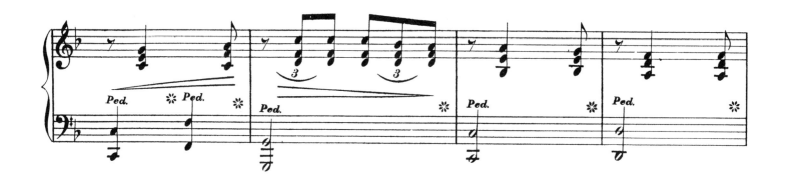

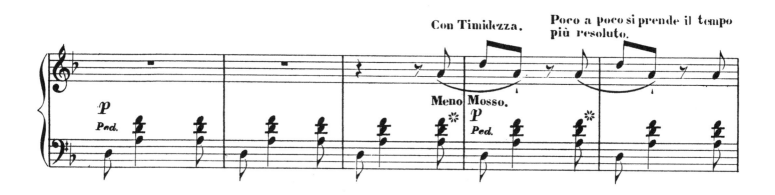

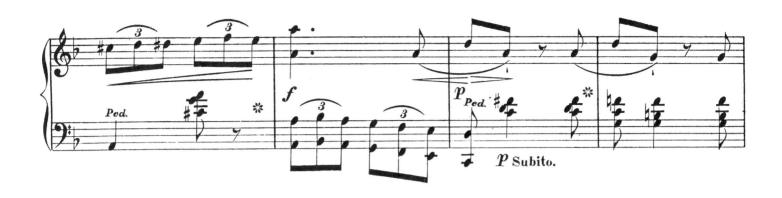

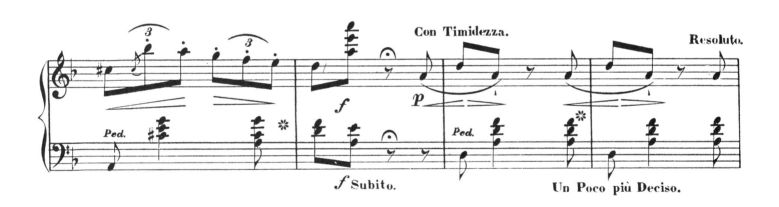

The Banjo

Grotesque Fantasie, American Sketch (1854–5)

Louis Moreau Gottschalk

Facilité.

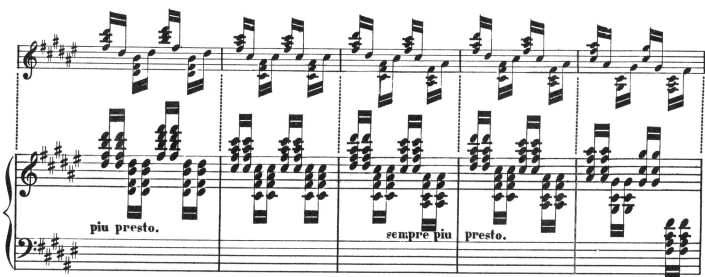

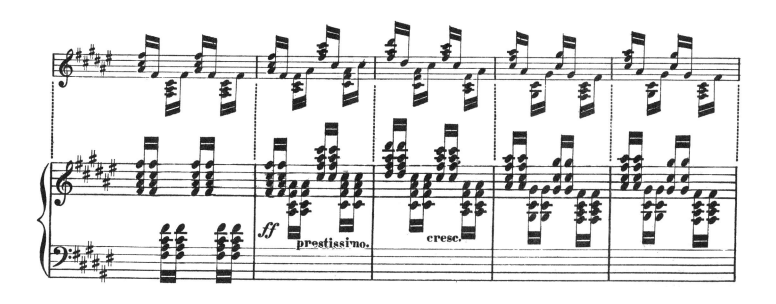

Three Tone-Pictures, Op. 5

Charles Tomlinson Griffes

EPIGRAPHS

(The Lake at Evening)

. . . for always . . .
I hear lake water lapping with low sounds
by the shore . . .

William Butler Yeats
From *The Lake Isle of Innisfree*

(The Vale of Dreams)

At midnight, in the month of June,
I stand beneath the mystic moon.
An opiate vapour, dewy, dim,
Exhales from out her golden rim,
And, softly dripping, drop by drop,
Upon the quiet mountain top,
Steals drowsily and musically
Into the universal valley.

Edgar Allan Poe
From *The Sleeper*

(The Night Winds)

But when the Night had thrown her pall
Upon that spot, as upon all,
And the mystic wind went by
Murmuring in melody—
Then—ah then I would awake
To the terror of the lone lake.

Edgar Allan Poe
From *The Lake: To—*

To Leslie Hodgson

The Lake at Evening

No. 1 of *Three Tone-Pictures*, Op. 5 (1910, later revised)

Charles Tomlinson Griffes
(1884–1920)

The Vale of Dreams

No. 2 of *Three Tone-Pictures*, Op. 5 (*ca.* 1912)

Charles Tomlinson Griffes

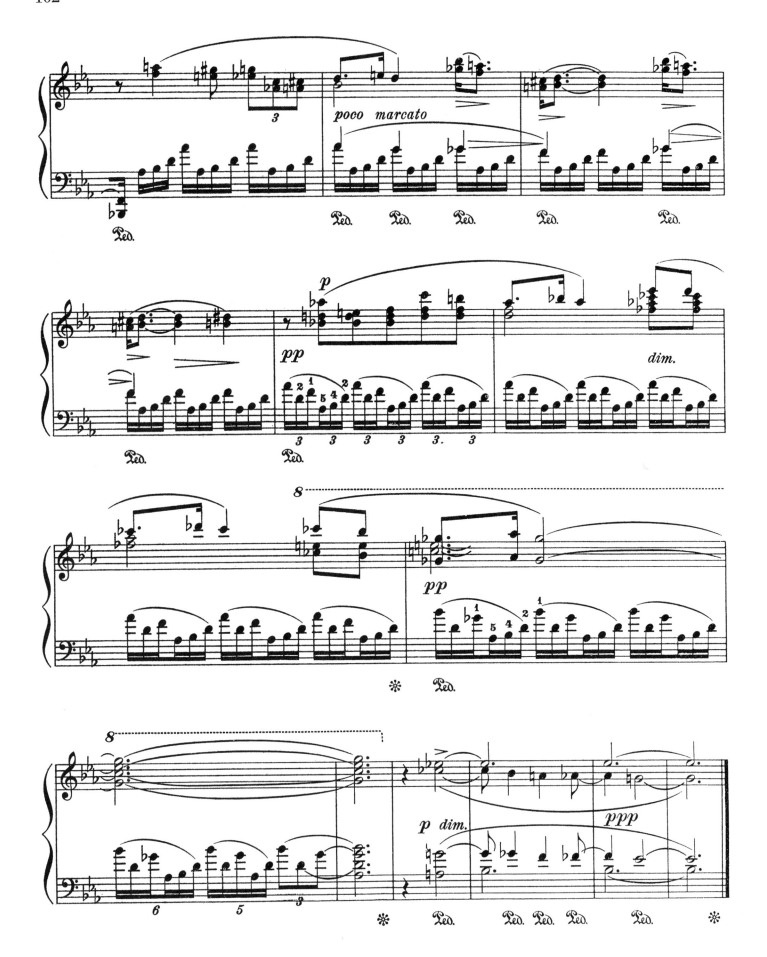

The Night Winds

No. 3 of *Three Tone-Pictures*, Op. 5 (1912)

Charles Tomlinson Griffes

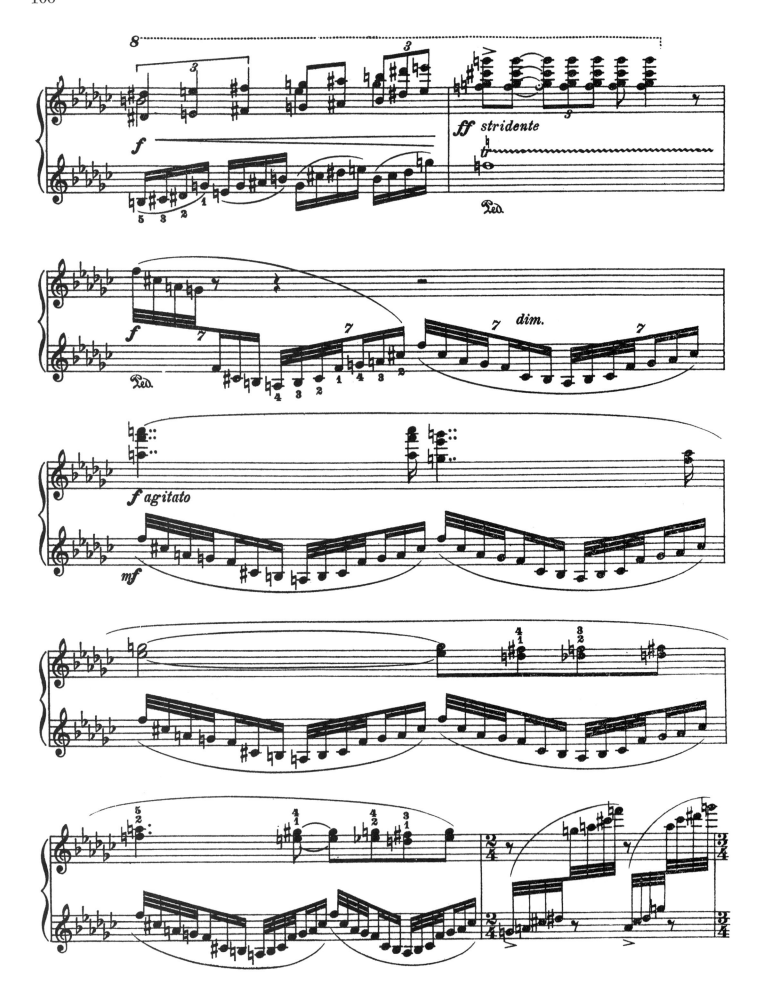

Sheep and Goat

"Walkin' to the Pasture"

Cowboys' and Old Fiddlers' Breakdown (1922?)

David Guion
(1892–1981)

Gaily, with marked swing and rhythm, though not too fast

Clog Dance

(1922?)

Howard Hanson
(1896–1981)

Rather fast, with marked rhythm

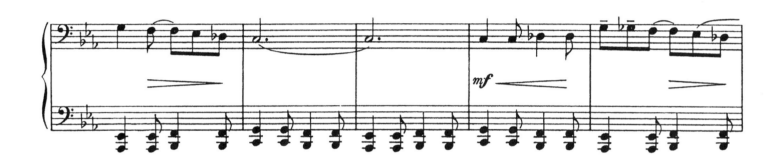

La Coquette

From *Six Piano Pieces* (1900)

Victor Herbert
(1859–1924)

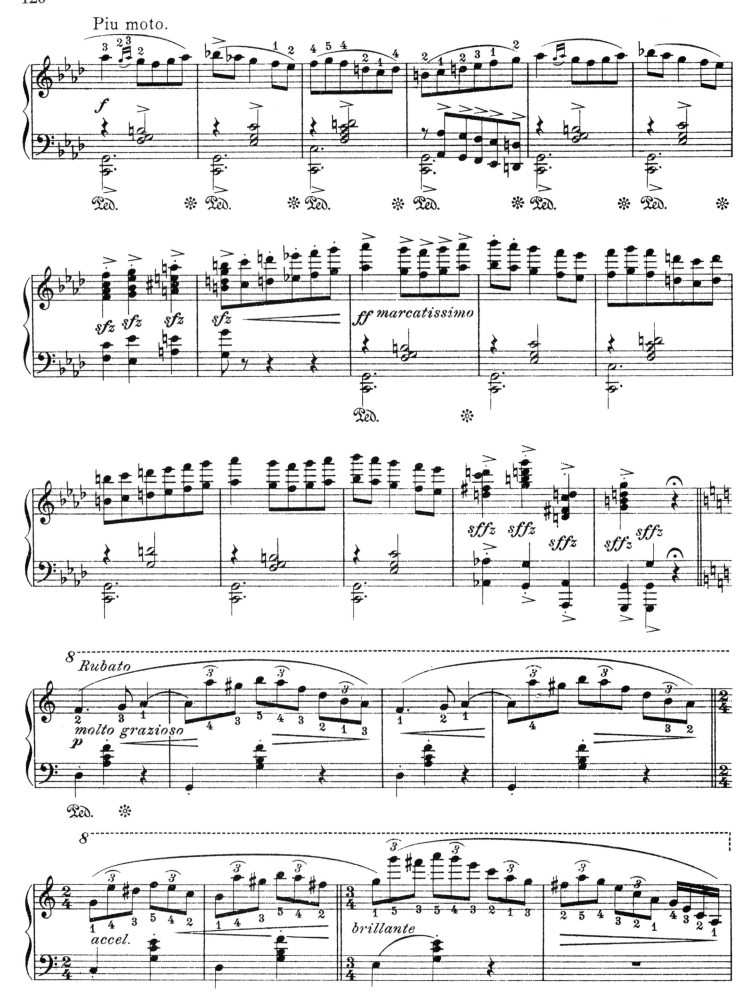

Indian Summer

An American Idyl (1919)

Victor Herbert

125

Fig Leaf

A High Class Rag (1908)

Scott Joplin
(1868–1917)

NOTE: Do not play this piece fast.
It is never right to play "Ragtime"
fast.   *Composer.*

Slow March Tempo

Bethena

A Concert Waltz (1905)

Scott Joplin

Ragtime Nightingale
(1915)

Joseph Lamb
(1887–1960)

Slow March Tempo.

138

The Land of the Loon

"A Camp-fire Story" from *Adirondack Sketches* (1922)

Eastwood Lane
(1879–1951)

The Joy of Autumn

The last of ten *New England Idyls,* Op. 62 (1901–2)

From hill-top to vale,
Through meadow and dale,
Young Autumn doth wake the world
And naught shall avail,
But our souls shall sail
With the flag of life unfurled.

Edward MacDowell
(1861–1908)

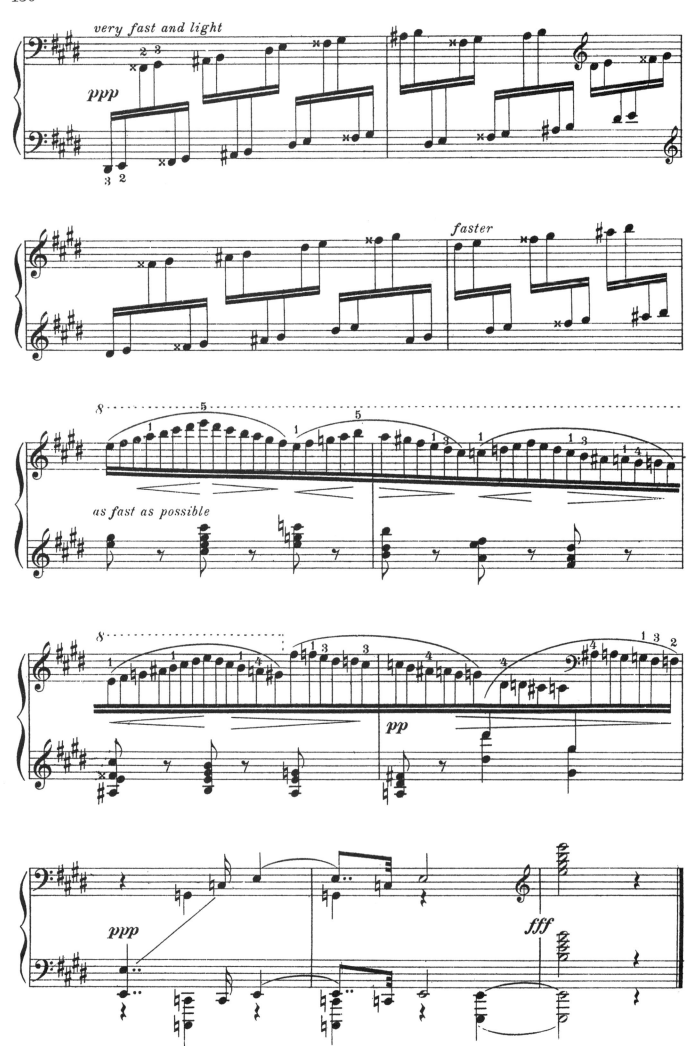

At Home

"June Night in Washington"

No. 4 from *En passant*, Op. 30 (1899)

"Outside the garden / A group of negroes passing in the street . . . / Sing with voices that swim
Like great slow gliding fishes / Through the scent of the honeysuckle:
My love's waitin', Waitin' by the river . . . "
(Richard Hovey)

Ethelbert Nevin
(1862–1901)

Like a banjo.

Melody well marked.

Always staccato.

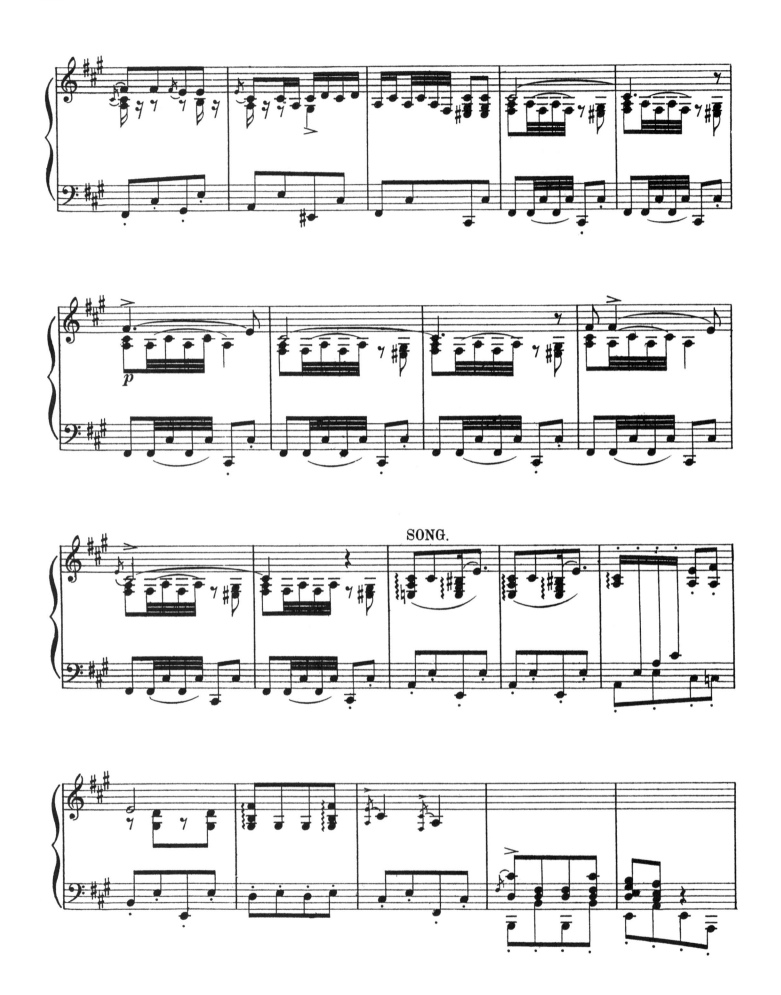

SONG.

QUARTET.

slower and more softly.

Birthday Impromptu

No. 2 of *Three Pieces*, Op. 41 (1882)

John Knowles Paine
(1839–1906)

A MON AMI

Dance of the Dwarfs

No. 2 from *Dwarf Suite,* Op. 11 (1913)

Leo Ornstein
(b. 1892)

Meno Mosso
marcato

ALPHABETICAL LIST OF TITLES